Lucky 13
A Grandparent's Guide

By Kathie Rodkey
(AKA Grandy)

PublishAmerica
Baltimore

ISBN: 1-4137-9182-4
PUBLISHED BY PUBLISHAMERICA, LLLP
www.publishamerica.com
Baltimore

Printed in the United States of America

Dedication

This book is dedicated to all of those grandparents who are raising their grandchildren. The dynamics of being a grandparent are altered significantly when a grandparent assumes full responsibility for their grandchildren; it creates an extremely challenging situation both physically and emotionally. You are my heroes.

Acknowledgments

Thanks to my wonderful husband, Tom (AKA Pap), my partner in watching the grandchildren, for his love, patience and dependability. My heartfelt appreciation to my children: Tommy, Christine, Kathy, Jeff, Daniel, Janice, Tom and Kellie for making it so easy for us to watch the grandchildren. Last, but not least, because I do not have a computer in my home, a special thanks to my computer angels at the Frederick County Library, for their patience in helping me with all of the technology aspects of this project.

Table of Contents

"A rotten day with the grandchildren is still 100% better than a good day in work ever was."
—Kathie and Tom Rodkey

Chapter 1
Physical and Mental Health

Physical Health

"Where is Grandy?" Hannah, two, asked Pap.

"Do you mean that nasty blonde lady?" he said.

"She's no lady," Hannah replied.

"Oh, yes she is, she's an old lady," her cousin Candace, four, yelled to her.

Owen, four, informed me that his sister Caroline, eight, told him that she thought I would still be alive when she got married. I inquired of Owen if he thought I would still be alive when he got married. After a long pause, he said with a very sympathetic look on his face, "I don't think so, Grandy, sorry!"

The most important thing you can do for yourself is to eat healthy, not smoke, limit alcohol, get plenty of sleep, and see your doctors regularly. A healthy body will result in a healthy mind, and you will need both to enjoy your grandchildren to the fullest. I did not mention exercise because you will get plenty of that if you watch the grandchildren regularly, take them for walks, and participate in their play activities.

I will not say another word about your health after this section, but I truly believe that the essence of quality of life is to take care of yourself physically. You cannot hope to be in a good position to help with your grandchildren and to really enjoy them without good health.

Mental Health

When I talk about good mental health, I am hoping that by the time you are a grandparent that you are in a peaceful place. By this I mean you like yourself and that you are no longer negatively impacted by what others say to you or about you. It is a fact that grandchildren can be brutally honest with their comments, so you must have good self-esteem and not internalize anything they might say. The following is a good example of such a situation. Olivia was four years old when I heard her say, "Grandy, you have such pretty yellow hair." I was just about to say thank you when she said, "It matches your teeth."

At least Olivia and I were by ourselves when she decided to comment on my hair and teeth; not so for Pap. Candace was three when she decided to brush Pap's hair, even though her parents were entertaining and the room was full of people. Suddenly, she pointed to the bald spot on the back of his head and said loudly for all to hear, "Pap, why do you have two foreheads?" Ironically, four years before this incident, when Olivia was five, she was brushing Pap's hair when he pointed to the bald spot on the back of his head and asked jokingly if she had brushed that. She replied exasperated, "I can't brush it, Pap, it's just like a forehead."

And the comments don't stop when they reach a certain age, as evidenced by the following. I have to admit I did set myself up for this one. I appeared in front of Olivia, who was 11 at the time, with all of my hair pulled back in a bun and inquired as to how she liked my hairstyle. There was a very awkward quiet moment during which Olivia made several very negative facial expressions, after which she finally said, "Gee, Grandy, I don't mean to hurt your feelings, but the more hair you have covering your face, the better you look."

Pap fell into the same trap when he and Candace, four, were watching television one day.

"Candace, do you think that Pap is handsome?"
"Oh, no, Pap," Candace replied.
"Then do you think I'm ugly?" he asked.
"No," she said after a long pause.
"Well, if I'm not handsome and I'm not ugly, what am I?" he pressed on.
"You are nothing, Pap," she tentatively replied.
"Nothing? You think that I am nothing?" he said with astonishment.
"But you are a whole lot of nothing," she quickly replied in a very relieved voice.

The bottom line is that I was first in line when whitening products for the teeth came out, and I do wear as much hair around my face as possible. Poor Pap, however, hasn't been able to do much about his two foreheads. He is very content to be a whole lot of nothing, though.

Another key to good mental health is to truly understand that to be healthy is more important than anything else in life. Whenever the grandchildren complain about their circumstances, I remind them how bad sick people have it and threaten to take them to the nearest hospital so they can see for themselves. When they start to complain and I am around, they stop quickly and look at me and say, "We know what you are going to say, Grandy." Unfortunately, for many people it takes a prolonged and serious illness to make them realize how important it is to be healthy. I have witnessed the lives of loved ones and friends changed instantly due to unforeseen tragedies, so embrace each day with joy and face each obstacle with calmness and you will be so much happier mentally, not to mention nicer to be around. A stressed-out, picky, uptight grandparent is no fun.

Another situation that seems to have an impact on the grandparent/ grandchild relationship is the grandparent's job situation. Of course, for those grandparents whose jobs are still a priority or necessity, they have less time to devote to the grandchildren. This is not so much of an issue unless, when they visit with the grandchildren they are so distracted because of job stress that they lose a very important element of the relationship, and that is the ability to give the grandchildren their undivided attention during the entire visit. So if you are still working, leave the job behind when you visit your grandchildren. My experience indicates that one hour of quality time with the grands will be more memorable than seeing you on a daily basis, while you are distracted. If you are preoccupied with something else, they can sense it immediately. Also, if you are working just to buy the grandkids material things, keep the following in mind. Candace, three, got a new toy from her parents. As with all children nowadays, this is a frequent occurrence. We asked her if she thanked them, to which she replied, "Why?" We said because they work very hard to buy things. We went on for at least five minutes explaining how people work to get money to buy things and that the more things they buy the harder and longer they have to work. When we were finished, she looked at us solemnly, put her hands up in the air, and replied, "Well, what's the use of that?" Ironically, I have found that children prefer personal attention to material things that they quickly lose interest in.

Not being afraid to admit your limitations and using your age to your advantage is also important for good mental health. I am a grandparent and proud of it. Even though I try to keep myself in good shape and dress with care, I have accepted the fact that I am aging and that there are certain things I cannot do. For instance, my lower back is very weak, so I must always be careful when I lift the children. I am not afraid to discuss my age with the grandkids, and I absolutely love being called Grandy, especially in public. It is a badge of honor I wear proudly.

"Abigail, I can't pick you up anymore, I'm weak and older than dirt," I said.

"Are you older than mud too?" Abigail, four, replied with concern.

The most critical element regarding your mental well-being is that you are not interested in controlling the lives of your children. During our years of babysitting, we have not had any arguments with our children. I believe this is due to the fact that my husband and I strongly believe that our role is to help our children by providing loving and dependable childcare, thus making their lives less stressful. If you feel that by babysitting you will be able to exercise more control over the way your children conduct their lives, then you will not have a successful or rewarding experience babysitting the grandchildren. The relationship between grandchild and grandparent is a special one based on different dynamics than those that exist between parent and child. To interfere with the parent/child relationship in any way other than to preserve the integrity of the parents will cause serious problems. Your first loyalty is to your children. Remember, also, that even innocent comments can be misinterpreted by the grandkids.

Owen, five, and I were playing basketball; mostly it was Owen running around, of course. I said I had to stop for a minute to put clothes in the dryer, and Owen followed me into the laundry room, upset that his game was interrupted.

"Why are you doing the laundry anyway, Grandy?"
"Because I like to do laundry and it also helps Mommy out."
"Why can't Mommy do that?" he said in a huff.
"Because Mommy is busy with her job and has to spend a lot of time on the phone."

When my daughter walked through the door that evening, Owen immediately told her, "Grandy said you don't have time to do the laundry because you spend too much time on the phone!" Luckily, my daughter, who is very easygoing, laughed and waited for me to fill her in on the exact scoop.

Another example of how you must watch what you say occurred while I was waiting for Owen to get home from kindergarten one day. I felt ambitious enough to clean the floor of my daughter's basement, which was dirty from a flood and resultant repair work. When Owen got home he noticed right away and commented on how good the floor looked. Instead of just saying thank you, I made the mistake of ranting about the amount of dirt I got up from the floor, how we were tracking it all to the upstairs, and that I hoped his daddy wouldn't cut wood inside the house anymore so that I wouldn't have to clean the floor again. All I can say in my defense is that breathing all that dust must have warped my brain. When Owen's father called home from a business meeting, Owen got on the phone and without even saying hello, said to him, "Daddy, Grandy said you can't cut any more wood in the basement. You have to do it outside so you don't make a big mess in the house again!" I can't imagine what it feels like getting out of a stressful business meeting, calling home, and listening to your five-year-old tell you what you can or cannot do in your own home. Fortunately for me, my daughter had already talked to her husband about that very issue, so I got off easy that time. However, if you can't say anything totally positive in a situation, don't say anything at all.

Finally, and this is of critical importance also, it is essential to get rid of all of your expectations. This not only applies to what you believe in your mind you will get from babysitting your grandkids, but also applies to your entire life. The happiest people I know are those who have no grandiose notions regarding what they will get in return for doing certain things. They also have no preconceived ideas of what people owe them in return for what they do for them. Spend time with the grandchildren for yourself, and only because you thoroughly enjoy doing it, and not because of any other ulterior motive.

In closing this chapter, if you truly are having difficulty getting to a peaceful place in your life, please get in touch with me and we can talk.

Chapter II
Hygiene and Safety

Hygiene

"See this toy?" Candace, two and a half, said to her daddy. "Pap's going to clean it. He's going to clean everything when I leave."

Of all the issues connected with babysitting our grands, it was paramount to follow certain hygienic practices, especially when at one point we were watching eight children ranging in age from a few weeks to five years old. The following are our steadfast rules:

A. Wash your hands thoroughly with soap and hot water, especially after changing and disposing of diapers. If you are outside with no toilet facilities, use a clean diaper wipe and make sure to get under your fingernails. I can't tell you the number of times my husband and I saw people change diapers without washing their hands afterward. There is only one word for it, and that is disgusting.

B. All children should wash their hands immediately after coming inside from outdoors, from school, before eating, and after going to the bathroom. They should wash their hands with soap and hot water until they complete singing one verse of any favorite song. Diaper wipes are an essential item for washing hands when toilet facilities are not available. Also, if your grandchild is a thumb sucker, make sure they wash their hands more often.

Hannah, three, and I are in the restroom at a local restaurant washing our hands. Keep in mind that Hannah has the loudest voice of all of our grandchildren. She sees a lady come out of the toilet and head for the door. She says loud enough for the woman to hear, "Grandy aren't you going to yell at that lady? She didn't wash her hands!"

C. Supervise toilet activities. In most cases, children under six need supervision in the bathroom to make sure the right amount of toilet paper is used and that they clean themselves properly. Girls should be taught early to clean themselves from front to back and boys to wipe the head of the penis with toilet paper after they are finished urinating. Both grandparents can help with this up to the age when children begin to ask for their privacy in the bathroom, usually about five to six years old, and sometimes younger, depending on the maturity of the child. Pap has wiped many a grandchild's rear end and applied lotion to many of their rashes, but at a certain age children will ask for privacy and you must hope that the lessons you have given on hygiene will be followed. If you suspect that they have not washed their hands after using the bathroom, feel or smell their hands to make sure they have done so. They will try to avoid washing if they think no one will notice, especially if they are in a hurry.

D. Dispose of diapers in separate plastic bags and carry them immediately to the trash outside. With so many little toddlers running around, we wanted to make sure that if they did get into the trash at least they would not make contact with dirty diapers. Also, it is unsanitary to keep diapers inside the house for days, not to mention the smell. I found that even the diaper container that enfolds each diaper in plastic began to stink after a few days.

E. Do not kiss children on the mouth. I realize this is an emotional issue, but I feel very strongly about it. It is not in anyone's best interest to kiss a child on the mouth. Affection can be shown just as effectively with a kiss on the cheek and a big hug, thus preventing the exchange of viruses and bacteria. My husband came down with frequent colds and viruses while babysitting, and I related it to his habit of kissing the children on their mouths. After switching his kisses to their cheeks, he got sick a lot less. On the other hand, I did not miss one day of babysitting because of an illness. I credit this to not kissing them on the lips or at all if they are showing any signs of illness. It is also important to keep their hands and fingers out of your mouth, as this is a surefire way to pass on bacteria and viruses to you. Remarkably, two of our grandchildren had not taken an antibiotic before the age of five, and in this day and age that is considered almost unheard of.

F. Do not eat children's leftover food. We do it without thinking, but this needs very little explaining in that it is also a sure way to catch whatever they may have or be getting. It is also not a good idea to let the children share each other's food or drink.

G. Keep pacifiers, bottles, thumbs, fingers, sippy cups and security blankets clean. I think if a child needs a security item, it is very unwise to force them to give it up before they are ready. I see many adults with their fingers constantly in their mouths and wonder how early they were made to give up a pacifier or bottle or were prevented from sucking their thumb. One of our grandchildren was taken off the bottle very early as her mother read somewhere that doing this would ensure healthier teeth. Interestingly enough, when she was five years old this same grandchild had to have a tooth pulled and several cavities filled. She was the only one of our grandchildren to have such extensive dental work at such a young age. I believe that brushing the teeth and gums twice a day as soon as they come in is much more important for dental health, especially if the child is born with a tendency toward soft teeth. Make sure all security items are kept clean by sterilizing the bottles and pacifiers and keeping blankets clean. Mold easily forms on the stoppers inside the sippy cups, so remove the stoppers from the sippy cups and wash them separately. Scrub bottles thoroughly before placing them in the dishwasher. If they are in the dishwasher for hours or days before cleaning, no amount of washing is going to destroy the mold and bacteria that has already formed.

H. Wash all toys frequently with hot water and soap. If a child has a fever, cold or other illness, wash the toys they were playing with as soon as possible and frequently during the illness. This hogwash about children needing to be deliberately exposed to dirt and germs to build the immune system is ridiculous. Children are exposed to plenty of germs in their daily activities and while playing with other children without exposing them to illnesses because of lack of hygiene. I firmly believe that the more viruses a human gets, especially while they are very young, the more the immune system is compromised for life. I also feel that frequent use of antibiotics also seriously compromises the immune system. Antibiotics should never be used for anything but a confirmed bacterial infection. Viruses, such as colds, do not respond to antibiotics. Unfortunately, as well as flushing bad bacteria out of the system, antibiotics also deplete the good bacteria. If your grandchild is taking antibiotics for a confirmed bacterial infection and they are able to tolerate yogurt, give them some to replace the good bacteria they are losing. They should also be encouraged to drink plenty of water to flush the antibiotic through the system quickly, thus avoiding yeast infections, urinary tract infections and the depletion of their good bacteria. It is very encouraging that doctors are becoming more responsible about prescribing antibiotics only for bacterial infections.

I. Take the children's shoes off after they have been playing outside. Because children spend so much time on the floor, it is a good idea to remove their shoes. This will prevent dirt from being tracked into the house, and then eaten or played with by the infants sitting or crawling on the floor. Also, without shoes on they are less likely to hurt another child if they accidentally step on each other or make other contact with their feet.

Safety

We had just started working with some of the grandchildren on looking both ways before safely crossing the street the day that Owen, who was four, and I saw a dead deer in the middle of the road. A couple of minutes after we passed the deer, Owen said very solemnly, "That's what he gets, Grandy, for not looking both ways before he crossed the street." The following is a list of some of our most important safety rules:

1. Never leave children in a room by themselves. Make use of playpens (play 'n' packs), cribs, high chairs with safety straps, or strollers to confine infants or toddlers if you need to go to the bathroom, answer the phone or door, or for any other reason that may distract you from the child. Otherwise, children should never be left alone for even short periods of time. The grandchildren have not incurred a broken bone, stitches or any other serious injury while we were watching them, but we worked very hard to avoid injury. When the children were very young, either my husband or I were always in the room where they played. When only one of us was watching them, either the children accompanied us to the bathroom, or phones and doors went unanswered until all the children could be confined, and then for only short periods of time. Our most difficult days were those on which we had three infants and a couple of other children. It took the two of us and much vigilance to keep things under control.

2. Check on sleeping children often. This is a safety issue on which I am adamant. We should never get so involved in other activities that we can't check on a sleeping child frequently. For me, the rule was every five minutes until they were asleep, and then every 15 minutes after that. All excess toys and pillows should be removed from the crib or pack 'n' play before the child goes to sleep. Many children require a favorite stuffed animal or blanket to fall asleep, so checking on these children frequently is also a must. Because blankets with breathing holes in them are the safest, try to introduce this type of blanket early on if it appears that they will need a blanket as a security item. I can assure you that you do not want to be responsible for the cleanup involved when a child you presume is sleeping has removed their dirty diaper and is spreading its contents all over the crib and walls. Many babies seem to have a bowel movement shortly after being put down for a nap, possibly because they are relaxed. Checking on them frequently will also ensure that you can get to a dirty diaper before they fall asleep and end up with a rash. Also, some babies will not sleep with a dirty diaper, or wake up shortly after falling asleep; thus, discovering it as soon as it happens will ensure that they get a good nap.

Olivia was three and just about out of the nap phase when I put her and her newborn sister Caroline down to sleep in separate rooms. At 2:30 p.m., I passed Olivia's room and she said, "Grandy, what are you doing?" I told her I was checking on her sister. At 2:45 I passed her room again and she said, "Grandy, what are you doing?" I again told her I was checking on the baby. At 2:55, I passed her room again and she said somewhat annoyed, "Grandy, what are you doing now?" I again told her that I was checking on Caroline, to which she replied in a huff, "If you keep on doing that, I'm never going to get any sleep."

Caroline was five when I asked her if she had gone into her brother's room and woke him up, to which she replied defensively, "I did go into his room, but I promise I didn't get in his eyes."

3. Never put an infant or a toddler in a bed to sleep. Prior to the age of three, too many accidents can occur; namely, falling off the bed, suffocating in bedding, leaving the bed and wandering unsupervised around the house or even out-of-doors, and being hurt by other children who can reach them too easily.

Curtis, four, was sleeping overnight at our house. He was watching me as I was preparing the bed and placing a plastic protector under the sheets. He immediately inquired as to what the plastic thing was for. I explained to him that I was putting it on just in case he had an accident. He said, "Don't worry, Grandy, I hardly ever fall out of the bed anymore."

4. No jumping on furniture. Children love to jump on beds and other furniture, but it is just too dangerous to allow it on your shift. I do recommend to both parents and grandparents that if they have an old couch to put it in a play area so that the children can use it to make tents; however, as with any other type of play, this activity should also be monitored continuously.

5. Cut up all food in small pieces, and do this for as long as you can get away with it, no matter how old the grandchildren are. When one of our granddaughters was nine years old, she choked on a piece of orange, and I actually had to do the Heimlich maneuver to dislodge it. Just a few weeks before that, I dislodged a piece of food that another grandchild was choking on. Luckily, it dislodged just by slapping her

on the back several times. Hot dogs, grapes, carrots and apples are just a few of the foods that definitely need to be cut into small pieces before serving to children. I also recommend that you take a class on lifesaving techniques

6. Teach the meaning of danger both inside and outside of the house as early as possible, even before they can walk. Children understand a lot more than we give them credit for. By two, they should recognize the danger from fire in the fireplace, lit candles, lit matches, from the stove, etc.; the danger from knives, scissors and other sharp objects; the danger from animals, especially those they do not know; the danger from open windows; the danger from water; and on and on. Shortly after two, and especially when they begin playing outside, they should be taught to look both ways before crossing the street, stopping at the end of the driveway or other recognized boundary, and wearing helmets while riding bikes, scooters, skates or motorized toys. Our favorite word of warning was the word danger itself, and the grandkids would even say it to each other as soon as they could talk.

7. Other safety issues:

A. Make sure you have the appropriate legal child safety seats in your car to transport the children.

B. As soon as they can write their name, teach them their phone number and address.

C. With consent and discussion with the parents, talk to the grandkids about strangers and what to do in certain scenarios. When the children were older, we would test them by knocking on the door and pretending to be a stranger to see if they would open the door. We would quiz them on their telephone numbers and addresses and what they would do in case they got lost, which was to stay exactly where they were. We also tested them on what they would do if a stranger offered them candy and how they would react if a stranger told them that mommy or daddy were hurt and that they had to come with them. Many times, our grandchildren failed these tests. Their parents will, of course, have the main burden for teaching these issues, but if you are watching the children frequently or on a full-time basis, you will get involved. Don't ever assume that your grandchild would never go with strangers and that this issue does not apply to you.

D. Cover all electrical outlets.

E. Don't let small children get anything out of the refrigerator by themselves.

F. Use caution loading and unloading children from cars, especially in parking lots.

G. Don't let children play on stairs.

H. Always supervise children on swings and slides, in swimming pools, and all outdoor activities.

I. This is non-negotiable! All children must wear helmets when riding bikes, skateboards or other motorized equipment. Believe me, they will resist, but you do not want to be responsible if a grandchild suffers a severe brain injury or worse while you are watching them and they are not wearing a helmet.

J. Insect repellant is a necessity these days with the mosquito population on the rise. Also, avoid dressing both the children and yourself in white clothes on picnics or walks in the woods as deer ticks are extremely attracted to white.

K. Teach the grands how to react to lightning and thunder if they are caught outside during a storm. Warn them of the dangers of standing under a tree during a storm. Teach them the squat position with their hands over their ears, not on the ground, to avoid being struck with lightning. Alert them to the importance of seeking shelter as soon as the weather looks threatening, not when thunder or lightning has already started.

L. Last, but not least, make sure there is a fire escape plan from their residence that they are aware of and have practiced; that they know how to stay close to the floor and near a window if they are trapped in a room with smoke; and are taught the stop, drop and roll technique if they are on fire.

As I finish this chapter, I am heartbroken to hear that two little boys are in critical condition with severe burns because of an accident that happened while they were alone. On your shift, be sure to supervise all of the children's activities. There is definitely an emotional difference between accidents that happen when parents are caring for their children versus those that occur while grandparents or other caregivers are in charge. One of our grandson's broke his leg because he was jumping off the ladder leading to his slide, something that we had warned him about and prevented him from doing on our shift. If it had happened while we were caring for him, we would have felt absolutely awful. We certainly didn't worry as much about or feel as hyper about injuries occurring while we were raising our own children as we do now that we are watching the grandkids.

In closing, do not commit yourself to watching more children than you can comfortably care for. As a grandparent, you will be more stressed over having a child hurt on your shift. Unless you have a partner or other type of assistance, you can only safely handle a certain amount of children, so don't overextend yourself.

Chapter III
Stages

Infants: Newborn to Age Two

Schedules are very important as all children, especially infants, thrive on regular meal and nap times. It is also a good idea for grandparents to rest during this time to be ready for activities when the baby wakes up. Again, be sure to check on the baby frequently. If I am watching only one infant, while it is sleeping I read the newspaper, a book or magazine as it gets me off of my feet and relaxes me.

Suspect a food allergy if a baby is very fussy and has gas or consistently loose bowel movements. For many babies, the enzyme which breaks down milk has not activated by birth, and they cannot tolerate milk. There are a variety of formulas that are good alternatives in these cases. One of our granddaughters had a very serious allergy to milk for the first year, but after that she was able to tolerate dairy products.

Take the baby for walks outside. The fresh air is not only healthy for them, but also for you. There are really only a very few days during the year when you cannot spend some time outside. Always put a hat on the baby to protect it from the sun and wind. Hats with ties are advisable, as most babies resist keeping a hat on.

Always put your grandchild to sleep in a parent-approved position. If the parent wants the baby on its side, then this is the way it should sleep. Be prepared to stand guard over the baby if you change the position for some reason. Our first grandchild was one week old when her exhausted mother asked us to watch her while she attended a wedding. I observed as the baby tried to fall asleep on her side, noticing that she would sleep for a couple of minutes, then jump as if she had been frightened, and wake up crying. Knowing that the baby was also completely exhausted after a week of not sleeping well, I made the decision to put her on her stomach to see if it helped. I pulled up a chair and, with the exception of bathroom breaks, basically watched her as she slept for six hours. She woke up refreshed and ravenous; however, I was exhausted from the strain of watching her so that she wouldn't stop breathing while she was on her stomach. My daughter came back to a happy, refreshed baby and asked how I did it. I was honest with her and told her about changing the baby's sleeping position, but she was not pleased with what I had done. It wasn't long before our grandchild chose by herself to sleep on her stomach. Now that I am a more experienced grandmother, I realize that I should have waited until mom was less exhausted herself and more experienced before telling her of this major deviation. New mothers and fathers can be very rigid about certain child care procedures, and we must try our best to respect their feelings.

You will not have any control over this issue, but in my experience, breast-feeding, in most cases, is very difficult for everyone involved. We actually saw no difference in the overall health of breast-fed versus formula-fed grandkids, but many people feel breast-feeding is very important. Some of the difficulties arise because breast-fed babies eat on demand and mothers must pump if they expect a grandparent to feed the baby. We actually know of cases where the mother went out supposedly for just a short while, got delayed and grandma had nothing to feed the baby, because the mother did not pump. Talk about a stressful situation. Also, if the mother eats such forbidden foods as chocolate, garlic, spices, broccoli, tomato sauces or drinks alcohol, the baby can really suffer. When my grandson was born, his mother developed a blood clot from the birth process. While his mother was in surgery, I watched in amazement as he gobbled up a two-ounce bottle of formula that the neonatal nurse was giving him. The next day he had no problem breast-feeding and continued to do it successfully for almost a year. Babies are a lot more adaptable than we realize. I believe mothers who pump have the greatest success with breast-feeding. This allows the father and other people to feed the baby while they rest or go out for a while. It also makes it easier on grandparents, knowing there is enough food to get them through their shift. Again, you must go along with the parents' wishes as long as they are reasonable and the baby is not suffering. If you are caught short of breast milk because of an emergency, giving a hungry baby a small amount of water in a bottle might help until the mother gets home. Another difficulty with breast-feeding is that mom doesn't know how much milk in ounces the baby is getting. Some babies become so exhausted sucking that they do not get enough to eat before they fall asleep and wake up 20 minutes later ready to eat again. Baby bottle nipples are easier to suck from, and so the baby eats more before it gets tired and generally sleeps longer between feedings. I find it is also beneficial to know exactly how much milk the baby is getting during a feeding to make sure they are thriving, and this cannot be assessed while breast-feeding. I do believe that breast-feeding is wonderful, but in all of my experience, it is much more successful for mom, the baby and any other caregivers if mom is willing to pump. Whether you are taking on full-time care of a newborn or just watching them on occasion, if they are breast-fed it is essential that the mom pump so that you have enough food to get you through your shift. As for giving infants their first solid foods, the parents will generally set the timetable for starting this process. We had a few grandchildren who could have eaten a steak dinner at three weeks old, and they went on cereal pretty quickly, because mom and dad needed some rest from the demands of a baby who was always hungry.

"Olivia, what is Caroline doing?" I asked.

"Eating Mommy's ninnies again, that's all she ever does."

Remember to change positions often when holding infants or you will end up with neck, shoulder, back and wrist pain. When lifting, bend at the knees. Speaking of holding infants, it is better for the baby and for you if you limit holding to feeding and alert times. It is also best to allow an infant to fall asleep in its crib. We had several grandchildren who had difficulty going to sleep, and one of them realized very early on that her crying could manipulate her parents. At three, she was still causing them many sleepless nights because she cried until they relented and let her in their bed. Her mother would end up sleeping on the floor all night or retreating to the child's bed. However, when I watched her and put her down for her nap, I let her cry a couple of times until she fell asleep, after which she never gave me a problem when she went for a nap or to bed at night. Children are smart enough to quickly adjust to different expectations of them, and thus the way they act with their parents is often different from the way they act around their grandparents. We have another grandchild who is a Type-A personality. As a baby she could be totally exhausted, but would fight sleep. She actually needed a good cry before she became exhausted enough to fall asleep. Every child is different, but I think it is worth it to allow a child to exercise its lungs for a reasonable time before they go to sleep, as long as they are well fed, have a clean diaper, and you know they are tired. Check on crying infants and toddlers frequently to make certain they are not in trouble, but try to wait them out. If they know you will eventually give in when they cry, the battle gets worse as they get older. Even a colicky baby can be soothed by rubbing its back or stomach while it is in the crib.

Be sure to keep extra clothes, diapers and bottles on hand, especially if you watch your grandchildren in your house. Invariably, you will need them because of a forgotten diaper bag or an accident or sickness resulting in soiled clothes.

Toddlers: Ages 2-3

They are up, they are down, they are happy, they are sad, they are crying, they are giggling hysterically, they are hugging and kissing, they are kicking and biting, and all in the space of a half-hour. Be prepared to be loved and hated many times during the day. This is the age when the difference between the way they act with grandparents and their parents becomes very obvious.

"Caroline, who is your favorite smurf?" I asked her the day she turned three.

"The mean one!" she replied.

Owen was three when he gave his mommy a picture he had just finished coloring. A few minutes later, I arrived to watch him for the day. As soon as he saw me, he took the picture from his Mommy's hand, gave it to me, and said to her, "This picture is really for Grandy, and you can just dream about it, Mommy."

The following are some helpful suggestions for dealing with toddlers:

Regular nap times are just as important for toddlers as infants. Those that took a nap until the age of three tended to be healthier and less cranky.

Toddlers are natural grazers. They like to eat small amounts of food frequently during the day, which is actually a very healthy way to eat. We cut up mainly fruits and vegetables and other healthy foods and offered it to them as they played. Most of our grandchildren were eating table food before they even had teeth, and Cheerios and applesauce were initial favorites. We also found that there is a very limited time period when children will eat baby food and, once they got a taste of table food that usually was the end of the baby food. Sometimes we had to mix the fruit and vegetable baby food together just to get a child to eat it. Another trick was to keep a bottle of formula, milk or juice handy and put it up to the child's mouth. When the child opened its mouth for the bottle, we would instead put a spoonful of food into it. We successfully fed one little fussy eater like this for months. It is always a pleasure to deal with a child that eats well, but the fact is that the majority of toddlers are very picky. Our expectations of how much they should eat are also sometimes unrealistic. I have seen parents put a bowl of cereal in front of a child that even a truck driver couldn't finish. Small servings are much better. Toddlers also like a variety of food. If you give them the same foods every day, they will reject them very quickly. On the other hand, they do go through stages where they will only eat one thing. Offering them cut-up foods frequently throughout the day also helps to give them a more well-balanced diet. On one occasion, two of our grandchildren ate a red pepper, a green pepper, a carrot, a peanut butter and jelly sandwich, a yogurt, a bowl of string beans, a peach, and two peanut butter cups while they were running through the sprinkler in their backyard. All of the food was cut up and they would run over for something to eat each time they came out of the sprinkler. Our favorite mealtime activity was setting up a fast food drive-in restaurant outside. Each child took turns coming up to the restaurant in their little play cars. When they arrived at the window, they had to choose a food item and pay for it. The food we went through during those games was unbelievable. We found that all of the grandchildren, no matter what the age, seemed to eat more on the run than they did sitting down at the table. Again, I can't stress enough the importance of cutting up their food in small pieces.

Outdoor activities are even more essential for toddlers. Being outside increases their appetites and allows them to get rid of pent-up energy. Make sure to apply sunscreen, put on their hats and make them wear sunglasses. They will also sleep better when they play outside in the fresh air.

Toddlers prefer playing with adults more than their toys. I can remember Pap and I spending an hour at a kitchen table spinning quarters while the children sat fascinated. They love playing with couch cushions and an old couch is worth its weight in gold in a playroom. Old blankets, sheets or pillows or anything that they can use to make a tent is very popular. I think we underestimate the ability of toddlers to learn. We started working on writing names at two years old. The key to success is not to pressure them into long amounts of time doing any one thing, as they do have short attention spans. A couple of the male grandchildren were not ready for name writing and other educational pursuits until they were much older than two. As toddlers, the boys tend to be more physical, affectionate and easygoing, while the girls mature quicker mentally but tend to be more complicated emotionally. Another interesting fact is that toddler children play better in pairs than they do when a third child is introduced into the mix. Boy and girl toddlers play well together, but at the age of about four, and definitely by five or six, they begin to prefer playmates of the same sex.

This is the age when children begin to behave differently with people, depending on expectations. Parents are busy with their careers, household chores, feeding the family, social obligations and other issues, and children realize quickly that if a parent is distracted they can get away with a lot more. On the other hand, when we watch our grandchildren we are usually in the same room and see exactly what is going on. So, when children fight with each other we usually know who the culprit is and which child is in need of a reprimand. Because parents are so busy, they sometimes do not see many of the rule breakers. Please keep in mind that my husband and I are healthy, mobile, active grandparents who could keep up with the rigors of watching several toddlers. We were also babysitting together most days, so there was always one of us in the room, and the children were aware that they couldn't get away with much. We always made it a policy to leave as soon as possible when our babysitting shift was over to allow the family to get into their own schedule. The longer you stick around, the harder the transition period is. Disciplining grandchildren is generally easier for grandparents because children tend to behave better for grandparents than they do their parents. Still, there will be times when you will need to enforce discipline. Children act up when they know that adults are vulnerable or distracted. Some examples are while shopping in a crowded store, talking on the phone, or having a conversation with another adult. In order to mete out fair discipline it is a good idea to talk to the grandchildren about your expectations of them in certain situations and what the repercussions would be for bad behavior. Our most successful method of discipline is to take away a favorite activity, toy, food, television program, etc. It is imperative, however, to follow through on the threatened punishment, so it should be something reasonable and yet something that will have an impact on the child. If you are not consistent with your discipline, you can expect the child to act up under similar circumstances. Also, you must be consistent in what behavior you will tolerate; if you do not allow them to jump on the couch or bed on Monday, then it should not be allowed on Tuesday. Be careful of favoritism based on gender or age. Just because a child is the youngest does not mean that he or she is never at fault, and just because the child is a boy does not mean that he is always the aggressor in a situation. Even though both my husband and I very infrequently hit our own children while they were growing up, I firmly believe it is not a proper or successful form of discipline. It teaches the child that hitting is a way for them to react to adversity and may create a bully. For most children, it does no good because it is a way for them to get attention, even if it is negative attention. In these situations, the parent finds themselves hitting the child more and more without positive results. Taking away a favorite thing or putting the child in time-out is always more effective.

This is the age also when the mention of underwear or anything connected with bodily functions will cause hysteria. We call it the potty-mouth stage. After returning from a trip to Italy, we watched our videotape with Abby, our almost three-year-old granddaughter. Two weeks later, we showed the tape to Abby's parents. As soon as the tape started, and much to our shock, Abby immediately said, "Are we going to see the man with the big peepee again?" It took me a few seconds before I realized that she was referring to the statue of David that I had filmed. I had no idea she had even noticed it, not to mention remembering it for two weeks. Another example of the potty-mouth stage happened while Pap and Curtis, who was almost four at the time, took their first trip to a public restroom together. They were side-by-side at the urinals when suddenly Curtis looked over at Pap and said loudly, "Look at Pap's big wuu-wuu!" There were at least three other men in the restroom, and my husband was mortified. Toddlers will sit with each other in the bathroom and actually compare their poop. Candace was three when she asked me what kind of poop her cousin Annie had just had. I asked Candace how many kinds of poop there were. She proceeded to run down the list…corn poop; circle poop; long, long poop; chunky poop; hard poop; soft poop; slow poop; fast poop; short poop. I was sorry I had asked. On another occasion, four of the three-year olds were making their own pizza and one of the toppings included green food coloring. Candace and Abby put the green coloring on their pizza, and Owen immediately made a comment about how their poop was going to be green the next day. After considerable group laughter, Owen pointed to me and said, "And Grandy's poop is going to be old." He now had a hysterical audience and, knowing he was on a roll, he then pointed to Pap and said, "And Pap's poop is going to be very, very, very old." They were rolling on the floor with laughter by this time. And for those of you who are now thinking that this is not very appropriate table talk, I say spend a morning with three toddlers and by the time lunchtime rolls around you pick your battles with regard to how rigid you will be. I also believe to completely forbid this kind of talk in the privacy of the home, when it is age appropriate, will cause it to resurface in other inappropriate venues. All of our toddlers went through the potty-mouth stage, but by the time they were four they knew what types of comments were inappropriate in certain situations. This might be due to the fact that they were allowed some freedom to have fun with an age-appropriate behavior. I feel that because toddlers have so many serious growing up issues on their plate, it is extremely important for them to have a good belly laugh occasionally with things that make them laugh. Before ending this section on the potty-mouth stage, I have two more stories.

"Owen, how was the ride?" I said as he disembarked from the roller coaster.

"It tickled my peepee, Grandy!" he replied with a devious grin on his face.

Thomas, who was fully trained at two years old, was going to the bathroom at a fast food restaurant. He searched for his penis, which he could hardly get his fingers on. When he finally found it and was barely able to hold it, he looked up at me with a big smile on his face and said, "Isn't this huge, Grandy!"

The following are some examples of how entertaining and smart toddlers can be. Abby was only two years old when she walked over to the refrigerator and said "Grandy, do you want a caffeine-free Diet Coke?" These were the exact words she heard her mom say to me every time I came into her house.

I was always telling the grandchildren to use the magic words please and thank you. Candace was just about four when she informed me indignantly that please and thank you were not magic words at all, but just ordinary, every day words.

Candace was two and a half when she was listening to the radio and heard a political announcement in which the candidate said something like, "You know me," as part of his advertisement. Candace immediately started crying and sobbed, "But I don't know him, Pap!"

"Grandy, you look tall tonight," Owen said as I walked into his house.
"And you look short," I said before realizing he didn't like my comment.
"But, Grandy, I look young and you look old," he immediately shot back.

Thomas was only two and a half when he got out of his crib about 10 p.m. one night. My daughter saw him and inquired as to what he was doing up. "What are you two still doing up watching TV?" he asked her indignantly.

"Grandy, Owen is teasing me," Candace, three, complained.
"Just ignore him, don't let him get your goat," I replied.
"I don't want her goat, Grandy, I want her horse!" Owen yelled to me.
I am always saying it is a free country when one of the children

doesn't like what another child is saying or doing, especially if it is not really impacting the other child. Owen's sister was making faces at him one day, and he started to complain about it. I started to say to him that it is a free country, but before I got the words out, Owen said, "I know what you are going to say, Grandy, but it is not a free country because everything in it costs a lot of money."

When Caroline was three, she had a habit of tuning me out when I called her. I would then raise my voice and call her by her first and middle name, which is Caroline Noelle. One day she got mad at her sister and said, "Olivia Noelle, why aren't you listening to me?" Of course, Olivia's middle name is not Noelle, but to Caroline, the word Noelle was what was added to everyone's name if they were in trouble.

So enjoy the show as your toddler grandchildren will be a constant source of entertainment. The following are some examples.

Owen was the first grandson born after we had four granddaughters. Caroline was three and a half when she watched mommy change Owen's diaper and saw a penis for the first time. She pointed to it with an amazed look on her face and asked her mommy what it was. Her mommy explained that because he was a boy he had a different peepee from her. Caroline looked closely at it again, pointed to it and said loudly, "Then why doesn't Daddy have one of those?" Everyone in the room, including grandparents and great-grandparents, were rolling on the floor with laughter. Her daddy was in the kitchen and came running into the room proclaiming something to the tune of how he did have one of those or she wouldn't be here.

My daughter had overnight guests, which included my 30-year-old niece, Susan. Abby, three, said to Susan for all to hear, "You can sleep in Hannah's bed tonight, right next to my daddy." My red-faced daughter explained that since their son Thomas was born, her husband had been spending a lot of time sleeping in the extra bed in Hannah's room.

My daughter walked into Abby's room to wake her up. Abby, who was three, looked up sleepily and said to my daughter, "I guess you aren't going golfing today because you don't have your golf shirt on."

We were entertaining relatives and were quizzing the grandkids on what their parents did for a living. Pap asked Abby, three and a half, what her daddy did for work. She replied, "Plays golf." Pap said, "What does Mommy do for work?" She replied, "Plays golf too!" Actually, they own a very busy home improvement company.

My son-in-law and Owen, who was three, were calling each other names. Owen was still having difficulty pronouncing his L's. After going back and forth with names like fire engine, truck, airplane, poo-poo head, etc., Owen said to his uncle what sounded like, "You are a fag." We were all in shock until we made him repeat what he said a few times, and realized what he was actually saying was you are a U.S. flag. His inability to pronounce the "L" sound gave it a whole different meaning. It was shortly after September 11, and Owen was very preoccupied with all the flags that were flying, so it was not surprising that he chose to use this.

We were at a baby shower and one of the older guests was using a walker. As she passed us, Caroline, who was three, said in a very loud voice, "Why is that lady taking her bicycle into the bathroom with her?"

In closing this section on toddlers, I would like to give you some words of warning. Be careful watching children of this age, because this is the time when you are most likely to get injured lifting a heavy three-year-old. Make them walk by themselves as much as possible. Also, so you can keep focused while driving with the grandchildren, the best thing you can possibly buy is kid song tapes. As soon as our grandchildren were settled in the car, they would beg for their songs. Even our four- to six-year-olds enjoyed hearing and singing to favorite nursery tunes, and the babies as young as six months also responded to the kid songs being played. They really make car trips much more pleasant. See Chapter IV, Places to Go, for entertainment ideas for toddlers and children of other ages.

Preschoolers/Kindergarten: Four to Six

"Owen, how was your first day at preschool?" I asked.

"Well, we said God all day, and then before we ate our snack we said God again!"

Children four to six years old are my absolute favorite. Children this age are much easier for grandparents to take care of physically. This is also the age when all sorts of comments fly out of their mouth, and it is also the time when they test authority with verbal retorts that sometimes make a lot of sense. They are also inclined at this age to gravitate toward playmates of the same sex. When they do play in mixed groups, it is a good idea to keep an eye on them, and never let them play behind a locked door, for this is the time when they start to get very curious about their bodies and the bodies of other children.

Four- to six-year-olds also ask a lot of questions about life and death. I know that in this day and age, parents try to protect their children from what they feel is life's unpleasant issues, but I strongly disagree with that theory. Children need to know that not everything in life is always rosy, and that part of the cycle of life includes death. Once they ask a question, I try to tell them as much of the truth as I think they can handle. I am, however, extremely open and honest about my own mortality so as to make them view death as a natural process and to help them understand my limitations. We visit the graves of several of their relatives as often as possible, and they thoroughly enjoy putting flowers on graves and walking through the cemetery. I keep the subject light, don't obsess about it, and certainly do not scare them about the dying process, as evidenced by the following:

Our granddaughter Caroline was nine when she said, "Grandy, you and Pap are the nicest people in the world, so when you die I am going to take good care of your graves."

It was a month after Owen's paternal grandfather passed away when we visited his grave. Owen, who was five, ran quickly up to the gravesite. He pointed to the bare area on the ground where the casket had been buried, and said very seriously, "Grandy, did Pop kill the grass already?" During that same trip, I removed the built-in vase from the grave marker to put flowers in it. Owen immediately saw the hole which was now visible because the vase was gone. His eyes got bug-eyed, and he quickly stuck his head in the hole and said, "Grandy, don't put that thing back yet, I want to see if I can see Pop down here!"

On another trip to the cemetery, I got confused about how to get out.

Owen said, "Grandy, don't go that way, it's a dead end." I started laughing at his comment and couldn't stop. He wanted to know what was so funny, and so I explained as best I could that because it was a cemetery where everyone was dead, that every place in it was a dead end. He got it right away and started laughing himself. As we were leaving, he said, "Grandy I bet you are going to put that funny thing I said in my baby book, right?" Now, every time we go to the cemetery he tells me to be careful of the dead ends, and laughs himself silly.

Owen was six when he said, "Grandy, when you die I am not going to miss you, I am going to over-miss you."

Another poignant moment came when Owen was six and said, "Grandy, when you die if I have a basketball game and it is your funeral, I will definitely go to your funeral." I smiled to myself. About 15 minutes later, he said, "Grandy, I've been thinking about what I said about your funeral. I wouldn't want to let my team down, so if they were playing a championship game, I might not be able to make your funeral." I laughed until my stomach hurt.

Olivia was five years old when we were watching a movie about a child doing homework. I said, "Someday I can help you with your homework," to which Olivia replied, "Will you still be alive when I go to real school?"

The following are some examples of comments made by our four- to six-year-old grandchildren, indicating their increasing verbal skills.

Curtis, four, complained to Pap that his sister was in a bad mood a lot, to which Pap made a comment that ended with the statement, "All girls are like that." A few days later, Owen, six, inquired about why Candace was so mad, to which Curtis quickly replied, "Pap says all girls are like that."

Candace was four when I announced that she had five minutes before she had to leave for home. When I informed her that her five minutes were up, she said, "Wait a minute, it hasn't been five minutes. Daddy always let's me stay up for five minutes more at night and it is a lot longer than that."

Abby was four when she got a card in the mail for her birthday. She said to her mom, "Something's wrong. Where is the present that goes under the card?"

Owen was five when he asked me if I had watched a certain television show the night before, to which I replied that I had missed it. He said, "Why did you miss it, Grandy? It was on at 8 Central, 7 Pacific time."

Candace was four when she was trying on dresses she got from a cousin we will call Mary. As she modeled each one for me she announced that she didn't like any of them. Shortly thereafter, she came out with a dress on that she said she liked, so I asked her if she had gotten it from Mary. She said, "Oh, no, Grandy, I only get dresses from Mary that I don't like."

Owen was five and getting ready for school. His mother pulled out an outfit from the closet, and Owen looked at it, put up his hands and said in exasperation, "Oh, no, I'm not wearing those handsome clothes today, I want to be comfortable.

Abby, four, was taking a walk with her mommy when she looked up at her and said, "Mommy, you better stop walking on all those cracks or your back is going to break."

Curtis was four when he arrived home and saw new furniture in his parent's recreation room. When his mommy got home he said to her, with his hands on his hip, "How much did all this stuff cost?" When his mommy mumbled something about it being on sale, he said, "Does that mean you got it for free?"

We were in church and Owen, five, asked if he could go with me to receive communion. I shook my head no, to which he replied, "Don't worry, Grandy, I'm not going to take one of those mints they are giving out."

On another occasion, we were in church when Owen, who was five, heard the priest announce the name of one of our relatives as being ill. He said loudly, "Wait a minute, isn't he better yet? We sent him a get-well card a long time ago."

Candace was five when she was watching ballet on television with Pap. She said, "You know, Pap, that boy dancers in ballet just help the girls spin around and then take bows at the end."

One day I was on the phone talking to Owen's mother when he came up to me and pulled on my arm and said, "Please get off the phone,

Grandy. Mommy doesn't need your help, she's 38. I need your help. I'm just five years old and a little kid."

"Grandy, when I grow up I want to be a singer," Candace, who was five, announced.

"But I never hear you sing," I replied.

"Yeah, I know. I don't really like to sing. I guess I should be a model," she said.

"But models have to brush their hair a lot," I told her.

"Oh, well, I guess that's out too!" she replied.

It was Halloween, and I was telling Curtis how much I liked his costume when his sister Candace, who was four at the time, said with authority, "It's not a costume, it's his pajamas. Mommy and Daddy are too cheap to buy a real costume."

My daughter was admonishing my grandaughter Caroline, who was four, reminding her that the word stupid was not to be used in their house, to which Caroline replied, "Can I say stupid in someone else's house?"

I was talking on the phone to Curtis, who was four, about Ping, his cousin's pet turtle. I inquired casually about when pre-school started. He said indignantly, "Grandy, I really don't want to talk about preschool, let's talk about Ping some more."

"Pap and I spent the afternoon at the governor's house," I bragged to the grandkids.

"Who is the governor?" Owen inquired.

"The most important man in Maryland," I responded.

"I thought God was?" Owen said without hesitation.

Owen was almost six when he said to me, his directionally challenged grandmother, "I think we make a left here, Grandy. Do you know what a left is?"

And last but not least, there is the comment that we will always treasure from Caroline, age six, which she made when she heard us talking about politics. She said, "Are you talking about those dumbacraps again?"

Four to six is the age when potty-mouth talk becomes more serious. Some examples of what I mean follow.

"Daddy, I know what my penis is for but what are those two balls for?" Owen, four, said to his daddy as they were watching a football game. His daddy quickly jumped up from the couch and left the room to make popcorn. As far as I know, Owen still doesn't know what they are for.

My daughter was in the hot tub with her daughter Abby, who was four and a half at the time. They had both gotten haircuts that day. All of a sudden, Abby points to my daughter's crotch and says, "Who cuts that hair, Mommy?"

I was buckling six-year-old Owen into his car seat, struggling to get it between his legs and fastened. Without warning, he looked at me with a sheepish grin on his face, stroked my face and said, "That feels so good, Grandy." My fingers left that buckle real quick.

"Every time I got in Jessica's face today, she kicked me in the nuts," Owen, six, said.

"What nuts are you talking about?" I said casually.

"You know, these," he replied, pointing to his testicles.

"Where did you hear them called nuts?" I continued, playing dumb.

"They just look like nuts to me, so that's what I call them," he replied, and then was silently reflective for about a minute before I heard from him again.

"By the way, Grandy, I also call them balls because they look like balls too!"

Obviously, he learned this slang from an older cousin or his peers. Interestingly, Owen's increasing knowledge of slang words for his body parts didn't concern me as much as why I had missed Jessica kicking Owen several times, especially in the family jewels. This situation, however, is a perfect example of what can happen when you are taking care of a number of children. Jessica is the youngest of five children, plus I was watching Owen and one of my other grandchildren. My husband was helping, but left for a brief period of time for a doctor's appointment, so I was left by myself with seven children. When you are in a situation like this, you miss some things even if you are as vigilant as possible. My advice is to try to avoid being in this position if you can and, if you are, gather them all into one room and play a game or watch a movie until reinforcements arrive.

Pap was always telling Owen he had legs just like his daddy. When he was five, he finally said to Pap, "I can't have my Daddy's legs because I came out of Mommy's body." My husband quickly left the room, leaving me to explain to Owen in simple terms why he could have both his parent's characteristics even though he came out of his mommy.

"Grandy, what is my belly button for?" Owen, five, asked.

"That's where the umbilical cord was that fed you while you were inside Mommy."

"Is that thing still in there?" he asked with disdain.

"No, they cut it off right after you were born."

"Did you save it, Grandy?"

"No," I said.

"Why not? You save everything else about me," he replied indignantly.

I recently showed Owen his birth tape again and pointed out his umbilical cord, which he watched his father cut. He sat fascinated and riveted to the television screen.

It has been my experience that children are born with certain personality traits that do not change very much over time. If your grandchild is easygoing as an infant, most likely they will be an easygoing person. If your grandchild is a wide-eyed, restless infant, watch out! All of our grandchildren continue to exhibit certain personality traits that they had to some degree as infants. These personalities start to define themselves in a big way between the ages of four and six.

Caroline is the middle child in her family. She is ten years old as of this writing and has always been a very intense child.

My son-in-law is a high-level administrator with a very demanding job. I have never seem him lose his cool until he volunteered to bring four-year-old Caroline to pre-school one morning. Ten minutes later, my son-in-law came into the house with his crying daughter, both of them shaking. She had refused to get out of the car because she had a bump in her hair. He absolutely couldn't convince her to go into the school and couldn't fix her hair to her liking, so he brought her back home. We warned him not to stress himself by getting involved with her morning antics, but he had to learn the hard way. It is a sad thing to see a grown man reduced to tremors by a four-year-old, but very comical too.

Caroline is also extremely fashion conscious and an avid shopper.

My daughter came down the stairs dressed for work one morning, and Caroline, who was four, looked up from her breakfast and said, "Mommy, you're not going to go out looking like that, are you?"

"Caroline, guess what, I'm going to the beach!" Candace, two, said excitedly.

"You are so lucky, Candace, there are so many places to shop," Caroline, six, replied.

"I don't want to shop, I want to play in the sand," Candace cried.

"Gee, what's wrong with her?" Caroline said with all sincerity.

I was staying overnight at my daughter's house watching the grandkids. Caroline, five, came up to me after I had changed into my well-worn pajamas, proceeded to feel them for a long time, and said with a very disapproving face, "Your pajamas are so thin, Grandy!"

Owen is our competitive, comical grandchild, and at this writing he is seven years old. He is the youngest child in his family and the only boy. He is also extremely competitive and loves sports. If he doesn't become a comedian or go into professional sports, he is definitely going to be a lawyer because he can talk his way out of anything.

"The sun is driving me crazy," Candace, five, says to Pap.

"The sun is driving me crazy too, but much better than you, Candace," Owen, four, immediately announces.

Owen's daddy reminds him that he better be good because Santa is watching him. Owen replies, "It's not Santa I'm worried about, it's God!"

Owen, five, announced that he stopped picking his nose for good. I reminded him that I had just seen him doing it a minute before. Looking confident, he quickly replied, "I know, that's because I just stopped doing it right this minute."

Owen, six, tells his parents how lucky his hermit crab is to be spending time at Grandy's while they are on vacation. His daddy inquired as to why, and he said as he rubbed his stomach, "All that candy."

Owen's neighbors were moving. There are eight people in their family. We pulled up behind the moving van, and Owen, who was five, saw at least 70 blankets piled high in the back of the truck. Not realizing that they were being used by the movers to protect the furniture, and thinking they belonged to the family, Owen said in amazement, "Grandy, look at all the blankets they have; they sure must get cold a lot."

Granddaughter Abby is our perfectionist and worrywart. I can just picture her staying awake all night worrying about something or other. She is the oldest in her family and is seven at this writing.

Abby was six when she lost her first tooth. About four in the morning, she woke up her parents to inform them that the tooth fairy had not arrived yet. They had forgotten to take care of it before they went to bed. While mommy kept Abby busy, daddy slipped something under her pillow. The next morning Abby came running into the kitchen, waving her five-dollar bill excitedly. My daughter whispered a comment to her husband regarding why he had given her so much money. He whispered back that he did his best considering he was trying to find money in the dark at four in the morning with a six-year-old watching his every move. I don't think they had much success in convincing Abby that five dollars was a special treat for losing her first tooth and that she probably wouldn't get that amount for every tooth she lost.

Abby's teacher gave a quiz to the parents of her first graders during back-to-school night, to determine how well the parents knew their children. The children were given the same quiz early in the day so the parents could compare their answers. Except for Abby's name, my daughter got every question wrong. My daughter asked Abby's teacher if she recommended therapy for them! The next morning, my daughter discussed with Abby her disappointment that she had failed the quiz, especially as she thought that she knew all of Abby's favorite things. She continued the conversation by telling Abby that she thought her favorite color was lilac, not blue as she had put on the quiz, and that she definitely thought macaroni and cheese was her favorite food, not pizza, which was the answer on Abby's quiz. Abby quickly replied, "Oh, man, those are the answers that I wanted to put down, but I couldn't spell them." My daughter realized that her little perfectionist had decided to give answers to the quiz that she definitely knew how to spell, rather than risk misspelling the correct answers; so much for psychological testing. My daughter called Abby's teacher to let her know what Abby had done so she wouldn't think that she was clueless about her child. On a positive note, at least my daughter could read Abby's answers; some parents were not even able to read their child's handwriting to determine if their answers were correct.

Olivia, who is 13 at this writing, is our grandchild who needs to have everything under control. She is the oldest child in her family and was the oldest grandchild for many years until we welcomed four stepgrandchildren into the family, one of whom is a year older than Olivia. Olivia is very detail-oriented, knows everything that is going on with everyone in her family, listens to everything that is said, and follows instructions to perfection. She doesn't have a competitive bone in her body and is very easygoing when it comes to playing softball, doing gymnastics and diving. What stresses her out more than anything is being late for events. She is extremely sociable, but seems to be more comfortable as a follower, rather than a leader.

Olivia was four when she announced the following to some children she was playing with on the beach.

"Bad little boys and girls in my house get put in a closet with a little hole in it."

"Olivia, have you ever been put in a closet at home?" her mortified mother asked.

"No," Olivia replied unconvincingly, after a long uncomfortable silence.

My daughter apologized to the adults who heard the conversation and left the beach with Olivia. She immediately told her husband what Olivia said, and he started laughing. He told my daughter that when they first arrived at the beach condo, they saw a storage closet on the deck with a small hole in it. The men in the group started teasing Olivia, telling her that if she or her cousins were bad, that would be the time-out room. The next day my daughter tried to explain the misunderstanding, but she still felt that some of the people didn't believe her. Again, watch what you say! It may come back to haunt you at the worst possible time.

Olivia's detail-oriented personality showed itself in the following discourse.

"Olivia, doesn't that look like Pap's boat out there?" her daddy asked.

"Does Pap's boat have a top on it?" Olivia, five, asked after looking at the boat.

"No, it doesn't," he replied.

"Well, that boat has a top on it, so how could it possibly look like Pap's boat?" she asked in a huff.

Olivia's need for control, even with regard to the inanimate objects in her life, was evident very early on.

"Olivia, I think we should get a dog for the dollhouse people."

"I don't think so, Grandy, the dollhouse people are afraid of dogs."

"Pap will build a doghouse for it."

"Oh, no, Grandy, he has to build a cage."

"Why does it have to be a cage and not a doghouse?" I asked with curiosity.

"Because if it is in a cage it can't get out unless I let it out," Olivia, four, replied.

Candace, who is seven at this writing, is our strong-willed, artistic and creative grandchild, who loves nature and the outdoors. She has a mind of her own in all regards. There are two children in her family, a girl and a boy, and she is the oldest. When we took her fishing, even though she was supplied with a perfectly good fishing pole, she spent most of the trip making her own pole with a stick and piece of string she found. For her, an outing is more about the process than it is about the actual event or the end result. At this writing, she has her younger brother wrapped around her fingers.

Candace, six, was in school, and Pap was watching Curtis, four, at our son's home. Curtis had to go to the bathroom, noticed a sign on the bathroom door, and asked Pap to read it to him. Pap told him that it said, "Candace's bathroom. Do not use!" Curtis refused to go in that bathroom despite Pap reassuring him that it was everyone's bathroom to use. No matter how hard Pap tried to convince him, he insisted on walking up the stairs and down the hall to another bathroom.

One day, Pap took Curtis to the dollar store and bought him two boats. When Candace came home from school and saw the boats, she put her hands on her hips and demanded to know why she didn't get anything. Curtis quickly said with a worried look on his face and while pointing accusing fingers at Pap, "It's not my fault. I asked Pap to buy you something, but he said no."

Recently, we were at the beach, watching five of our grandchildren play. We noticed that Abby and Candace, both seven years old, were instructing the younger kids on what to do to get a sand castle built. The other children were working very hard running back and forth collecting buckets of wet sand. I inquired as to whether the two of them were going to do anything to help make the sand castle, to which Candace replied, "No, Abby and I are the princesses and they are our loyal workers." On the way home from the beach, we got into a discussion about the two of them ordering the little ones around, and both Abby and Candace said sincerely at almost the same time, "We aren't bossy at all."

Curtis, who is five at this writing, is our split personality. One minute he is affectionate, giving out hugs and kisses, and the next minute he is losing his temper over something. He is the youngest of the two children in his family. He is very thrifty, and puts all of his money in a wallet that he carries around. He is very lucky and finds money on the ground all the time; probably because he always has his head down looking for it. He still gets so excited, even if he finds just a penny. He is proving to be a very good athlete, and is an avid fisherman who can cast a rod as good as his grandfather. Pap has been waiting 40 years to get a fishing buddy and is thrilled that it has finally happened. Recently, Curtis caught a catfish and would not rest until Pap cooked it so he could see what it tasted like.

Curtis was three when he found a quarter on the ground. He said excitedly, "Look at this, Pap, I found a quarter and I'm going to save it to buy a condo just like yours."

On one of our many trips to the dollar store, Curtis, three, who was obviously tired of having his purchase combined with that of his many cousins, ran to the cashier first, slapped his purchase on the counter, and said "Separate bag, please!"

Curtis, four, was fishing with Pap. On this day, Curtis consistently left his pole on the ground, wandered around for awhile, came back, reeled the line in and pulled in a fish. Meanwhile, Pap was patiently holding his fishing pole without catching anything. After Curtis caught his fourth fish using his method, he looked at Pap and said, "I'm going to have to teach you how to fish the right way, Pap. You're doing it all wrong."

Curtis and Pap had just finished a trip to the local mall.

"Where are we going now, Pap?" Curtis asked.

"We are going to stop by your uncle's house," Pap replied.

"No, I don't want to do that, I want to go home!" Curtis cried.

"If we go home, you will complain that you are bored out of your mind," Pap said.

"To be honest, Pap, I'm bored out of my mind right now," Curtis replied.

Our grandson Thomas was talking in sentences at 20 months and fully potty trained by two. He is now a month shy of four but acts like he is years older than that. He is the only boy and the youngest of the three children in his family. Thomas is the only two-year-old I have ever known who could sit through an entire movie without moving. He swims like a fish and has been diving into the pool since he was two, even though he can't walk from one place to the other without tripping over himself.

"Thomas, you are such a silly billy," I said after he pulled one of his antics.

"I'm not Billy, Grandy, I'm Nicholas!" Thomas, who was only 22 months, teased.

Just recently, Thomas, three, entered the room where my daughter was entertaining a large group of people. He pulled on my dress and said loudly enough for all to hear, "Remember, Grandy, when we sat around at your house and watched me, Abby and Hannah take turns coming out of Mommy's peepee?" He was, of course, referring to the baby videotapes I took of each of them, which they watch frequently when they visit.

Hannah, who is now five, is the middle child in a family of three children. She is our easygoing, sensitive and extremely affectionate grandchild. She adores animals of all kinds and went through a period where she had at least five leashes, all of them in use on someone or something. She goes along with the crowd and never complains about a thing. She is usually in a world of her own as evidenced by the following story. The family dog, Bennigan, has been a part of Hannah's life since she was born. My daughter and son-in-law were going out-of-town recently and had dropped Bennigan off at day care. Yes, you read that right, I did not say kennel; there are now day care facilities for dogs. At dinner that night, Thomas inquired as to where Bennigan was, to which Hannah, five, replied, "Who is Bennigan?"

Abby, five, was taunting Hannah, who was three, teasing that she had a peanut butter cup and Hannah didn't. Normally, this type of activity would send a typical toddler into hysterics, but Hannah, true to form, just looked up at Abby and said in a carefree voice, and with all honesty, "I don't care."

My husband and I are blessed to have four beautiful grandchildren who also have very distinct personalities. Katie ı years old at this writing, and is the oldest in her family of five childrε She has an extraordinary talent for writing, and I am constantly blown away by her stories and poems. Lauren will be thirteen soon and is a very serious and sensitive child and a deep thinker. Nicholas, who is ten, is the only boy in his family, sandwiched between two sisters on either end. He loves outdoor activities, and does a great job of controlling himself, especially considering he is surrounded by all those sisters. Anastasia, six, is a social butterfly and clothes horse. She can change her outfit three or more times a day. My stepson's daughter, Jessica, three, is the most petite child we have ever known. She was late in talking, but now has an opinion on everything. She has her mother, father and everyone in her family totally under her spell.

Pre-Pubescent: Six to 12

Puberty seems to begin much earlier these days and, along with it, the mood swings. Challenges with homework, extracurricular activities and social issues begin to emerge. The relationship between the child and grandparent rapidly begins to change. Grandchildren become aloof, preferring to be with their friends over spending time with the grandparents. They also are busier with school and other events in their lives, which make them less accessible to grandparents. This is perfectly normal, and that is why my husband and I always advise people that they have a short window of opportunity to bond with their grandchildren and enjoy wonderful moments with them. No matter how busy our grandchildren become or how little we see them, nothing can break the bond that we have already forged with them during those all important first years of their lives.

Olivia was twelve when she asked her mother if she could spend the night and the next day at her girlfriend's house. I was due to babysit Olivia and her siblings the next day, and her mother inquired as to whether she would rather spend time with Grandy. She replied quickly, "Don't worry, Mom, it's really okay. I just saw Grandy last Sunday."

hen I saw Olivia every day; however, presently more without seeing each other due to our Ɪectations with regard to how often the older Ɪⱻ see me, and when we do get together there are no ꞮⱻⱮnents made with regard to not visiting or calling. Without ꞮⱼⱱDt, there are still many wonderful times ahead with the older grandchildren as they continue to entertain.

We were entering a park for a picnic and fishing expedition with seven of the grandchildren, when this incident occurred.

"Look at that sign. It says anyone over 63 doesn't have to pay," said Olivia, 11.

"That's me, an old fart," Pap replied.

"At least you are a free old fart," replied Olivia.

These days, helping the grandchildren with homework is stressful for grandparents because of all of the new methods of teaching.

"Olivia, please help me with my math homework?" Caroline, nine, implored.

"Okay, what is the math symbol I am pointing to?" Olivia asked.

"Oh, that's easy, it's a right angle," replied Caroline.

"No, it's not," Olivia said, exasperated.

"Then it must be a left angle," said Caroline, obviously very proud of herself.

The following was a very memorable verbal exchange which occurred during a visit to a fast food restaurant. We had noticed for a long time that Olivia was struggling with pre-pubescence issues, but during this visit she was in a very carefree mood, and we were delighted just watching her enjoy herself with the younger kids.

"Grandy and Pap, do you know what 'COOL' means?" asked Olivia, 11.

"I don't have a clue," replied Pap.

"It means a constipated, overweight, overrated loser!" Olivia exclaimed.

"I'm actually an 'ERK,' Pap," she continued.

"How do you spell that, and what does it mean?" Pap said.

"'ERK' means intelligent rich kid," she said proudly to Pap.

"But, Olivia, intelligent is spelled with an I, not an E," Pap informed her. "So, it should be 'IRK,' not 'ERK'!" he said, barely able to control himself.

Well, so much for the intelligent part of her assessment of herself. Her face was red, but she was able to laugh with abandon for about five minutes over that one.

Teenagers

This is the time when your unconditional love for your grandchild can be a blessing. Teenagers need someone to listen to their problems and not preach to them. By keeping your emotions intact and not being judgmental, your grandchild will be more inclined to tell you things that they might not dream of telling their parents. In this way, you may find out early something that needs the attention of their parents. Remember, again, that your first loyalty is to your children and that you must support wholeheartedly the decisions your children make with regard to their teenage child.

Do not take teenagers distancing themselves from you personally; it is a normal process in the hormonal phase. As the adult, you will need to be more aggressive in keeping in touch with your grandchild. At this age they seem to prefer one-on-one visits with you rather than group visits, especially if they include their younger siblings. A movie and lunch date or shopping trip for the female grandchildren works well, while the boys enjoy bowling, arcade visits and, of course, fast food stops as frequently as possible. Don't be discouraged if you don't get a return call or a thank you note, or if they frequently cancel out on meetings with you because of a better offer, as this is the height of the self-centered stage of life. Send them a card occasionally with a couple of dollars in it, especially if you haven't seen them for a while. Believe me, even if you don't get a response, these expressions of love will carry them through this tumultuous period in their lives and will provide them with good memories of you that will remain with them as long as they live.

On a more serious note, this is the time when your children need your support more than ever. In this day and age, the decisions facing our children while trying to raise their children are overwhelming. How much in the way of material things do you give them even though you can afford it all? How much extracurricular activity is enough even though you can afford to sign them up for everything? How do you emphasize academics, especially when social obligations are overwhelming? How do you make a decision on public versus private schools? How do you instill some type of work ethic when everything is geared toward having fun and many families have maids and gardeners? How do you warn them about all the dangers from drugs, alcohol, speeding, the Internet, early sex and possible resultant diseases and pregnancies, as well as certain people predators? How do you get them out-of-doors and away from all of the technology gadgets? How do you get them to exercise? How do you allow them to play in an unsupervised environment and still be sure they are safe? How do you get them to eat properly even though everyone is too busy for family meals? Last, but not least, how do you get them to listen and talk to you? If you criticize your children's decisions on how they raise their children, and interfere with decisions made by your children, you will soon find yourself ostracized. I have known some grandparents who find it amusing that their grandchildren come to them to reverse a decision made by a parent, or who deliberately sabotage a parent's decision by doling out money or items that the parents have denied. I am telling you that this is a very dangerous game to play and one that can have severe consequences for the family relationship and the well-being of the grandchild. If you are interfering in any negative way with the relationship between your child and their children, my advice is to step aside immediately or you will be very sorry in the end. If you have inside information from your grandchild on an issue you perceive to be serious, your obligation is to present it to the parents in a calm manner and try to help the parents work it out. On the other hand, if the situation involves abuse that is clear and well-documented, and the parent is unable to control it, then you need to be the child's advocate and get the authorities involved immediately.

Chapter IV
Places to Go

Infants

Usually, bringing infants anywhere is a chore for grandparents. Infant's moods are very unpredictable, so you may get someplace just as the baby becomes unhappy. For that reason, we found it better to stick close to home with infants. We took the babies for walks around the neighborhood every day for fresh air. When the babies became more alert and aware of people, we would walk through malls so the babies could "people watch." When the babies could sit up, we would go to parks with swings. Because we had three or four infants at a time, we did not do much in the way of play dates with other babies, as they had each other for entertainment. If you are watching just one infant, you may want to join a group so that the baby can interact with other children. Our local library offers a group activity for infants and toddlers involving storytelling and interaction with puppets, which is very popular. I think it is important for young babies to socialize as long as it is done on a reasonable basis, and certainly when the baby is rested and well-fed.

Toddlers, Preschoolers, Pre-Pubescent Children and Teenagers

FAST FOOD RESTAURANTS such as McDonalds and Burger King, in our opinion, are still the most popular place for toddlers. They can eat and play at the same time. The play areas are limited to children of certain heights and weights, so that bigger children will not get in the way of the toddlers. Be sure to have them wear or bring their socks, as they are required in the play areas. Gift certificates to these places are our favorite presents. The food is reasonably priced, and these chains have recently introduced healthier food menus. The kids like them for midday ice cream treats. On extremely hot days, it is wonderful to sit in the air conditioning and watch the kids play. Even the older grandchildren still enjoy eating at the fast food restaurants, especially when their pre-pubescent and teenage appetites kick in and they just can't seem to get enough food.

CHUCK E. CHEESE'S is very popular with toddlers, older children and adults. They have great pizza, drink refills, play areas and token games. It is much more expensive than McDonald's or Burger King, as the tokens go quickly, especially with older children and their grandfathers! The appearance of a live Chuck E. Cheese is always interesting, depending on the age of the child. On one visit, Candace, who was five at the time, said, "I sure wish we could find a Chuck E. Cheese with balls," as Chuck E. Cheese exited the stage. After further discussion with her, we realized that she was talking about the fact that the basin holding different colored balls that they could jump in had been eliminated from the play area. She had us going for a while. Chuck E. Cheese's is also a great place for a party. I noticed that some people actually brought their own birthday cakes, without going through Chuck E. Cheese's for their birthday package, which seems to be fine with the extremely child-friendly management. Watch for coupons in your local paper for good deals at Chuck E. Cheese's.

PARKS of all kinds are enjoyable, and children love change, so search them all out. Parks with lakes and trails are favorites. We lived in Frederick, Maryland, for three years before we realized that there was a fantastic nature park within a couple of miles of our house. Small water parks are being built in many places also, and the kids love them. Many parks have fishing holes for the children to use, which do not require a license.

NATURE WALKS OR GARBAGE PATROL WALKS are especially popular for children three to six years old. They enjoy looking for bugs, leaves and rocks, and even enjoyed picking up trash to make their neighborhood cleaner. Make sure to always bring a bag containing plastic gloves and garbage bags for collecting garbage, containers for storing the bugs, leaves or rocks that are collected, and bandages, tissues and wipes for the occasional accident that might require these items.

MUSEUMS are a great way to spend time with children five and up. We are very fortunate to live close to Washington, D.C., and its wealth of great museums; however, every state has interesting museums. For instance, in Frederick, Maryland, we have fantastic Civil War museums.

FAIRS are wonderful entertainment; however, I have learned the hard way that it is not a good idea to take children under four to a fair unless it is for a very short period of time. In most cases, you will be paying an admissions fee and parking rate, so you want to spend some quality time enjoying the entertainment. For this reason, we only take children five and over to fairs. The best advice I can offer with regard to fairs is to buy the discounted all-day ride passes. There is nothing worse than watching a young child lose it because they are out of their allotted outrageously expensive ride tickets after only a few rides. We generally arrive when the fair opens and stay until it closes. Every year, the grandkids cannot wait for their day at the fair. Look for advertisements for discounts on admission and ride passes, and don't even think of going without purchasing the all-day ride passes. Passes will make it easier on you because the grandchildren can get on a favorite ride as many times as they want, and you don't have to deal with the trauma of running out of tickets and spending more money than you would have if you had purchased the all-day ride passes initially.

FISHING AND PICNICS are a great way to entertain children of all ages. Again, as long as you keep in mind that a child's attention span is short and don't expect too much, an outing to a local fishing hole can be a lot of fun. Just recently, we fished off of a dock with five of the grandchildren. The two boys, both under five, happily held their rods, waiting for a fish to bite. The three girls, however, spent their time building a bird nest from weeds and other items they found at the site. They enjoy feeding bread to the fish and turtles they see, and have favorite local places they call Mr. Duck Pond and Mr. Turtle Lake. Some parks have boat rental areas and taking a ride in a boat is always a treat for the children. Again, make sure that the ratio of adults to children is comfortable for you so that safety is not compromised. Never go anywhere without a cooler filled with snacks and drinks, as children love to munch when they are out, even if they have just eaten breakfast or lunch.

POOLS AND SPRINKLERS, or any kind of water activity, including water balloon throwing, is a must activity for children during the summer months. It doesn't matter whether it is a small backyard pool or sprinkler or a sophisticated pool at a country club, kids love water. Again, be prepared for the munchies and bring plenty of snacks and drinks. Water parks are great for a change of pace but, again, we were more comfortable at water parks with the older grandkids only. You need to be extremely vigilant when watching the grandkids around water, so don't do any kind of water activity unless you can be totally in control of the situation.

BOWLING AND MINIATURE GOLF are great for children four and up. A mature three-year-old might enjoy throwing the bowling ball or swinging a golf club, but in our experience they don't last long before losing patience. Discount coupons for these activities are available and some bowling franchises even have honor cards for school-aged children, which gives them free games of bowling at certain times. Again, it is not advisable to bring toddlers, as the majority of them do not have the attention span or physical ability for these activities.

MOVIES are very popular ways to entertain the grandchildren, especially on rainy days. It is my experience, however, that young children do not do well sitting in a theater for an entire movie, no matter how child-friendly it might be. For children younger than six, renting a movie and making some popcorn at home is a better bet. When the children get restless or bored with the movie or need to go to the bathroom, the movie can be stopped until they regain interest. This method is also a lot less expensive than the price of admission to a theater and the outrageous prices of the food and drink. For children over six, a trip to the movie theater is a treat. If you are on a tight budget, plan to attend the matinees or movies before 6 p.m. because these are generally cheaper. Also, feed the children before the movie so you won't be mortgaging the house to pay for their treats. I often promise them a trip to a fast food restaurant after the movie or a stop at the local ice cream parlor so that they are not as focused on eating during the movie.

TRAIN, PLANE AND BOAT rides of any kind are a thrill to all-aged children. Paddle and row boats are available at local parks for rental. Be sure to get parental permission before you embark on these activities with your grandchildren. A helicopter or small plane ride is a thrill for a child who has never been in the air but, again, a parent's consent is absolutely necessary for this activity also. Another very entertaining activity for children is watching planes take off and land from a good vantage point near the airport. We are again very lucky to have several fantastic places to view planes in Washington, D.C., Virginia and Maryland. I will never forget the looks on the faces of our grandchildren the first time they witnessed a jumbo jet landing and taking off.

SHOPPING MALLS are a wonderful source of entertainment, especially when watching a variety of different-aged children. The following are places to visit and things to do:

PET STORES—just watching the animals pacifies most children. Occasionally, we will let them pick out a dog or cat to play with if the store is not too busy and the staff is agreeable.

CLOTHING STORES, etc. are magnets for the older grandchildren, especially the girls. Letting them leisurely shop in their favorite stores is a treat, even if there is no expectation that they will purchase or get anything.

DOLLAR STORES are great fun for the grandchildren, and we allow each one to choose one item per visit. It is one of their favorite activities and by the time they make their decisions, an hour has quickly passed.

PLAY AREAS—most malls have some sort of entertainment area in the form of small mechanical rides, carousels, play yards or arcades. We limit rides to one each as the last event before leaving the mall. We do not waiver on this rule so that there are no expectations for unlimited rides. We find that children do very well when they know what the rules are and realize that these rules will not be broken.

CIRCUS AND CONCERT activities are saved for our grandchildren over the age of five, as they have better attention spans and can enjoy the activity more. Concerts featuring popular young children's entertainers are okay for toddlers, as long as they are of short duration. Circus and concert activities are usually very expensive forms of entertainment and thus should be saved for a time when you know that the grandchild will thoroughly enjoy them, not to mention being able to remember the event. Offer to have your pre-teenage grandchild accompany you to a concert, no matter what the genre, or surprise them with tickets to a concert featuring their favorite pop star. The clock is ticking with regard to how much time they will want to spend with you, so be aggressive in setting up opportunities to be together.

LOCAL FARMS are a great place to visit with children. Horse farms, especially during the birthing season, are very entertaining and educational. Watch for advertisements featuring open house events, such as free rides. Be sure to tour the barns so that your grandchildren can see firsthand what it takes to maintain a horse. Agricultural farms are also wonderful sources of entertainment and education. Picking strawberries, peaches and apples helps to expend the energy they have as well as providing them with the best food sources. Several of our grandchildren's favorite memories of their late paternal grandfather is picking blueberries with him at a local nursery. He would then make a fantastic blueberry cobbler for them. As far as I am concerned, there is no better legacy to leave your grandchildren than memories like this.

BALLGAMES of all types are fun, especially as the children begin to participate in sport activities of their own. Even attending a cousin's all-star game can be exciting for the other children. After a recent softball game, Owen came off the field and bragged to his fan club, "Oh, well, I did hit a triple but unfortunately nobody could bring me in!" There is nothing more entertaining than watching five- and six-year-olds playing a sport for the first time, especially when it is your grandchild digging a hole out in left field completely oblivious of the ball rolling right by them. Again, we are lucky in our area to have so many professional teams to choose from, whose stadiums are in close proximity to our homes. Taking the children to sporting events at their parents' alma maters is also great fun. Allow time for the children to get autographs after the games from their favorite players.

LIBRARIES are fantastic places to spend time with your grandchildren. There is always some event going on, including wonderful storytelling sessions. Some libraries offer group activities for infants and toddlers that are very entertaining and educational.

I could just go on and on about things to do with the grandchildren both inside and outside the home, from doing crafts, to playing games, to organizing shows for their cousins, to visiting nursing homes, to collecting clothes and toys they no longer use or need and bringing them to designated drop-off points. The list is endless.

Chapter V
To Do's, Taboos,
Questions and Answers

To Do's

1. Definitely keep a separate photo album on each child. If you enjoy videotaping, individual movies on each child are also very popular. They love watching themselves on television, and have spent many hours being entertained by our tapes and photo albums.

"Guess what, I saw myself on television at Grandy's house!" Hannah, two, said excitedly to her mommy.
"Hannah, all of us kids are on television at Grandy's house!" Abby, four, replied.

2. Write down memorable comments immediately. As they get older, they enjoy hearing the things they said. Many of our grandchildren are always asking if we are going to put something they just said in their baby book.

3. Give the grandchildren your time. This book is not about how to help raise your grandchildren to get into an exclusive school or college; rather, it is about spending fun, relaxing time with them so that they will have meaningful, lasting memories long after you are gone. After about the age of 12, sometimes even before that time, grandchildren begin to distance themselves from you in favor of their friends, so it is important to establish a bond with them immediately.

4. If you watch the grandchildren in your child's home, leave it as clean as you found it. If you do extra chores such as the laundry or the dishes, don't brag or complain about it. Do these things only because you want to and not as an excuse to complain, or it will cause serious problems.

5. For birthdays and other special occasions, give the grandchildren bonds. Our children are fortunate in that they are able to provide nicely for their children, and so the grandkids have more than they need in the way of material possessions. Giving bonds assures that they will be able to buy something they really need when they are 18 or older. Have the bond mailed to your home so that your name is on it when you give it to the grandchild; in this way they will definitely remember your name. If you are worried about how bonds will go over at a birthday party, don't. The birthday parties held nowadays are so filled with gifts that no one takes notice of who gave what.

6. Leave the house as soon as your babysitting shift is over to allow the family to get back to their normal schedule as soon as possible.

7. Because we watched our grandchildren on a regular basis, we found that our children were sometimes reluctant to call on us to babysit for a special occasion. We got around this by giving the parents gifts of babysitting services. We found that the parents appreciated this more than material gifts.

8. If the parents can afford it, and you are babysitting full-time while

they work, charge them a reasonable amount. I found that even though we didn't charge anywhere close to the going rate for babysitting, that the exchange of money worked better for both parties. I believe part of the reason why the experience was so successful and lasted so long was because my husband and I never felt taken advantage of and the children felt better that they were reimbursing us in some way.

9. Discuss all issues of concern immediately with the parents in a calm manner. Above all, have total respect for the parents' wishes even if you are not totally comfortable with them. Your grandchildren are their children, not yours, and this difference is what makes being a grandparent so different and so special. The bottom line is that they are responsible for all the hard decisions which come with raising your grandchildren, and your most important goal is to support their efforts.

10. Tell the truth in answer to questions from both the parents and the grandkids and make these answers as simple and uncomplicated as possible, especially for the grandkids. Oh, okay, maybe your children too!

11. Discipline fairly and consistently. If children act out in public, calmly and immediately remove them from the area and follow through on an agreed-upon disciplinary action. All children must be taught at an early age that they cannot get away with tantrums, whether they are done in private or in public. I truly believe children need to know their limits and that their tantrums are cries for control. If you give in to them just to save face in an awkward situation, you have lost a very important battle which you will truly regret later on.

12. Maintain the best relationship you possibly can with your son-in-law or daughter-in-law, especially in cases of separation or divorce. Put aside all of your negative feelings and practice unconditional love. This will help your grandchild adjust tremendously to this very traumatic event in their life, and teach them that people can behave with respect toward each other despite differences. My husband and I

both have previous spouses, and we all gather together for special events and communicate often with regard to family issues. Our children and grandchildren have never had to make a choice about who to invite to an event because one parent couldn't be in the same room with the other. Keep in mind there are two sides to every story, so give as much support and love to both of your grandchildren's parents as you can, despite the circumstances.

Taboos

1. Never say anything negative about the parents in front of the grandchildren. If you put a child's loyalty to the test, it can tear them apart and eventually impact your relationship with both parent and child.

2. Never discuss a grandchild's behavior with the parents while the child is present.

3. Never rearrange the furniture or redecorate their homes.

4. Never cut a grandchild's hair or pierce any body parts without consent from the parent.

5. Never give a child medication or any kind of medical treatment without consulting a parent.

6. Never buy a child expensive toys or gifts or give them money without consulting the parent first.

7. Never open your children's mail or invade their privacy in any other way. Even though I always put the laundry away in the children's closets and drawers, I left the parent's laundry on their bed. Please keep in mind, laundry is one of my favorite chores, so I happily did it for all of the children when it didn't interfere with watching the grandchildren. So another taboo is definitely not to complain or brag about any chores that you do.

8. Do not discuss sensitive issues with your grandchildren without discussing the topic with the parent first to make sure that you are all on the same page.

9. There should be absolutely no hitting or verbal abuse toward the grandchildren. If you find yourself doing either of these things because you are watching them too often or because you feel stressed, you need to back off and reassess your commitment.

10. Do not overturn any decision a parent makes about your grandchild, whether you agree with it or not. Do not assist the grandchild in trying to defeat their parents or you will truly regret it.

Questions and Answers

To give you some more insight on my approach to grandparenting issues, the following are a just a few of the questions that I have been asked by other grandparents and the answers that I have given.

Q: **Our grandchildren have so much stuff. What is your suggestion for gifts?**

A: Bonds, bonds and more bonds. Have them sent to your home so that your name is on the bond. When the grandchild turns 18, not only will they have money to buy something they need, but there is the extra added bonus of having them know and remember your name. Also, make one parent the beneficiary, not the co-owner. As beneficiary, they cannot cash in the bond unless the child is deceased. If you designate them as co-owner, they can cash in the bond anytime. Also, in case the marriage dissolves, it is a good idea to make the beneficiary of the bond your son or daughter. A practical gift to buy the family is a small strong box with a key to hold the bonds. Remember, you will need the child's Social Security number to order bonds from the government.

Q: **Our children and grandchildren do not eat meals together. Any suggestions?**

A: There is not much you can or should do to interfere with the family dynamics. I personally feel that having dinner as a family is critical, as studies have indicated that children who have dinner with their families seem to do better in school and are healthier. Unfortunately, in this day and age, our idea of dinner every night as a family doesn't seem to fit into our children's busy schedules. I'm not sure that any harm is done to the children if the families eat together only a few nights a week versus every night, as long as they are getting attention in all other areas. Make sure that when you are watching your grandchildren for the day or overnight that you prepare a home-cooked dinner and have the grandchildren help you fix it and clean up.

Q: **We think our grandkids spend too much time watching television, playing video games or using the computer. What can we do?**

A: On your shift, plan other activities such as bowling, biking, tennis, hiking or playing ball. Our grandchildren were always eager to have us play any type of game with them. All of our grandchildren are computer savvy and a couple of them even have their own computers, but it was never difficult to get them away from the television or computer in favor of doing something with us. How much time they spend watching television or on the computer when they are with their parents is not your business.

Q: **Our teenaged granddaughter is so distant lately. What's going on?**

A: She's hormonal and is doing what is totally normal. This is why I say spend as much time with the grandchildren as possible in those early years. They grow so quickly and before you know it they prefer the company of their friends over both parents and grandparents. Once you have established a solid relationship with a grandchild, you will never lose that special bond even though they eventually distance themselves. Be sure to call and leave her messages of encouragement, or send a card reminding her how much you love her. Try to arrange a date with her to do something that you know she is interested in; however, never put a grandchild on a guilt trip over not seeing you or refusing to join you for an outing. Your teenaged grandchildren are going through enough turmoil without any pressure from a grandparent. This is the time to practice unconditional love.

Q: **Our 14-year-old grandson keeps asking us for money. It's hard to refuse him. What should we do?**

A: Don't give him any more money. Pick up the phone and talk to his parents immediately about the situation, including how long it has been going on and how much you have given him. You have no idea what he is doing with that money, and you do not want to be responsible if he is not using it wisely. In any case, this situation has to stop immediately.

In closing this guide on being a grandparent, I must tell you that one of my best friends finally became a grandmother recently to beautiful twin boys. I am thirteen years ahead of her in grandmother-hood, so she has had to listen to all of my stories for all of these years. I must have said to her a hundred times, "Just wait, Linda, you won't believe what it's like to be a grandparent." I would describe Linda as a consummate professional and a very controlled person in all she does; after all, she is a Virgo. We were talking on the phone recently, and she announced with complete sincerity and amazement, "I can't believe it, but I make a complete fool of myself when I am with my grandchildren." This quote says it all.

I hope that this guide will be helpful in accomplishing your goal of enjoying your precious grandchildren. Let me know if I can help in any way with either issues that I may not have covered or issues that I did cover. Contact me at P.O. Box 1319, Frederick, Maryland 21702-0319. Good luck, and enjoy the greatest gift life has to offer: your grandchildren.

CPSIA information can be obtained at www.ICGtesting.com
Printed in the USA
BVOW07s2217250913

332147BV00001B/29/P